Deleted

Deleted

We
Shall
Overcome

The March on Washington

Rachel Tisdale

PowerKiDS
press™

New York

Published in 2014 by The Rosen Publishing Group
29 East 21st Street, New York, NY 10010

Produced for Rosen by Calcium Creative Ltd
Editor for Calcium Creative Ltd: Sarah Eason
US Editor: Joshua Shadowens
Designer: Paul Myerscough

Photo credits: Cover: Corbis: Flip Schulke (fg), Library of Congress: Warren K. Leffler
(bg). Inside: Corbis: Bettmann 25, 27; Flickr: Stab at sleep 11; Getty Images: Robert
W. Kelley/Time & Life Pictures 24, Michael Ochs Archives 15; Library of Congress: 7,
13, Frederick Dielman 4, Ed Ford 12, Orlando Fernandez 3, 20, Carol M. Highsmith
Archive 28, Warren K. Leffler 1, 8, 10, 18, 22, Stanley Wolfson 16; National Archives:
White House Photograph Collection 19; Shutterstock: L. Kragt Bakke 9, Donald
Bowers Photography 5, Maximus256 14, Spirit of America 29, Jarno Gonzalez
Zarraonandia 21; Wikimedia Commons: Walt Cisco, Dallas Morning News 26, Cecil
Stoughton 17, USIA photo 23, John Vachon, Library of Congress 6.

Library of Congress Cataloging-in-Publication Data

Tisdale, Rachel.
 The March on Washington / by Rachel Tisdale.
     pages cm. — (We shall overcome)
 Includes index.
 ISBN 978-1-4777-6069-7 (library) — ISBN 978-1-4777-6070-3 (pbk.) —
 ISBN 978-1-4777-6071-0 (6-pack)
 1. March on Washington for Jobs and Freedom (1963 : Washington, D.C.)—
Juvenile literature. 2. King, Martin Luther, Jr., 1929–1968. I have a dream—Juvenile
literature. 3. Civil rights demonstrations—Washington (D.C.)—History—20th
century—Juvenile literature. 4. African Americans—
Civil rights—History—20th century—Juvenile literature. I. Title.
 F200.T57 2014
 323.1196'07309046—dc23
                                        2013026888

Manufactured in the United States of America

CPSIA Compliance Information: Batch #W14PK5: For Further Information contact Rosen Publishing, New York, New York at 1-800-237-9932

Contents

Unfair Treatment

Today, US citizens have the same legal rights as other citizens, regardless of race. This was not always the case. For almost 250 years, white European settlers brought Africans to America to work as slaves on huge cotton and sugar plantations in the southern states. The slaves were cruelly treated, and had no control over their lives.

The Abolition of Slavery

Although the United States abolished slavery in 1865, equality did not follow, and African Americans continued to be treated unjustly. Most of the freed slaves lived in the southern states, where the plantations were. Many freed slaves were killed,

African Americans all over the country celebrated when slavery was abolished in 1865. However, life did not improve for all former slaves.

All Americans today are free, but for African Americans this was not always the case.

tortured, and beaten for committing "crimes," such as attempting to vote, talking back to a white man, or even just for being unpopular.

No Opportunities

In the northern states, too, African Americans faced unfair treatment. Bankers would not lend them money to buy houses, which meant they had to live in the poorest areas of cities and towns. White people were reluctant to employ African Americans in good jobs, so most had to take low-paid work.

The NAACP

In 1909, the National Association for the Advancement of Colored People (NAACP) was formed to fight against the unfair treatment of African Americans. The organization, based in New York City, started to pursue equal rights for African Americans through the US courts. It went on to become one of the major civil rights organizations that helped secure equal rights for African Americans during the 1950s and 1960s.

Suffering and Segregation

Even 100 years after the abolishment of slavery, life for African Americans in the United States had improved little. Due to their involvement in slavery, many white Americans continued to have racist attitudes toward African Americans and did not see them as equal human beings.

African Americans had to drink from separate drinking fountains because of unfair segregation laws in the South.

Jim Crow Laws

African Americans still faced discrimination and abuse on a daily basis. Some white Americans, especially in the southern states of the country, wanted to keep themselves separate from African Americans. They were afraid of what would happen if everyone mixed freely. Southern states passed laws, known as Jim Crow laws, which stated that African Americans had to use different facilities from white Americans.

The Ku Klux Klan

The Ku Klux Klan (KKK) was an organization founded in 1865 after the American Civil War. It formed to fight against equality for former slaves and against African Americans being voted into southern state governments. The KKK eventually had members and active groups in all of the southern states. There, they waged a war of terror and violence against many African American and white American leaders and voters who were supportive of equality. During the civil rights movement of the 1950s and 1960s, the KKK was responsible for bombings in churches and schools in the South.

Separation

African Americans had to eat in separate restaurants, travel in different sections of buses and trains, and even enter some public places, such as movie theaters, through rear entrances. The facilities for African Americans were usually worse than those for whites. The laws of separation became known as segregation.

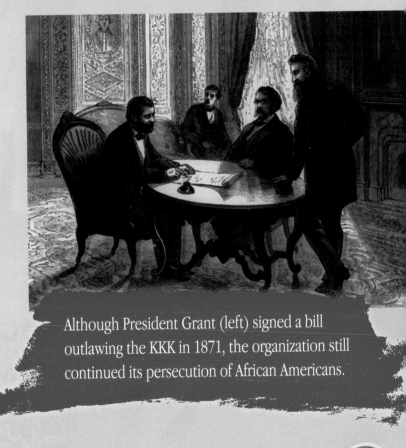

Although President Grant (left) signed a bill outlawing the KKK in 1871, the organization still continued its persecution of African Americans.

A True Leader

The struggle for equal rights gathered force in the 1950s and 1960s and became known as the American Civil Rights Movement. One of its most influential leaders was an African American pastor named Martin Luther King Jr.

Family Footsteps

King's grandfather was a minister in rural Georgia who then moved with his family to Atlanta, and took over the small Ebenezer Baptist Church. When King's

Martin Luther King Jr. became a prominent leader in the fight for civil rights for African Americans.

grandfather died, his father, Martin Luther King Sr., stepped in as pastor at the church. After doing well at school and college, his son, Martin Luther King Jr., entered the Christian ministry in 1948 and became assistant pastor at the Ebenezer Baptist Church.

Martin Luther King Jr. became assistant pastor at the Ebenezer Baptist Church, in Atlanta, when he was just 19 years old.

Civil Rights

Martin Luther King Jr. believed that through his congregation he could gather support for making changes within the community, and achieve his aim of equal rights for African Americans. King went on to become a key figure in the American Civil Rights Movement.

"He is the first to make the message of brotherly love a reality in the course of his struggle."
The chairman of the Nobel Committee on awarding Martin Luther King Jr. the Nobel Peace Prize in 1964.

Ending Segregation

In 1957, Martin Luther King Jr. invited around 60 African American ministers to meet with him and other civil rights leaders in the Ebenezer Baptist Church. Together, they formed a new civil rights organization, the Southern Christian Leadership Conference (SCLC), with the aim of ending segregation through nonviolent means.

During the 1950s, African Americans all over the United States joined the fight for equal rights. Those in the civil rights movement organized mass protests, and took test cases to court to argue for equal rights for African Americans.

"There lived a great people, a black people who injected new meaning and dignity into the veins of civilization. This is our challenge and our overwhelming responsibility." **Martin Luther King Jr.**, speaking during the Montgomery Bus Boycott.

Education for All

In 1954, the highest court in the United States ruled that it was wrong that several African American children were denied entry into white schools. This became known as

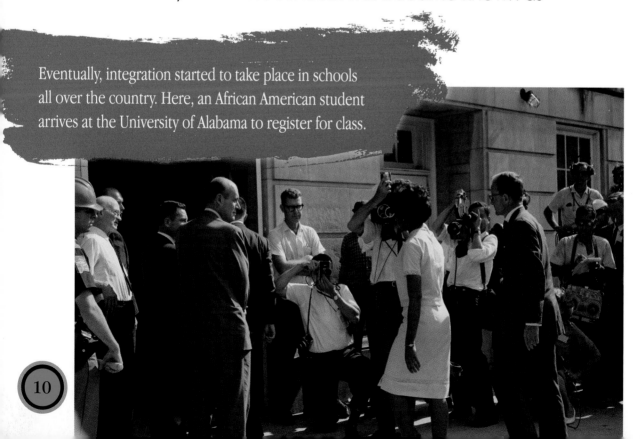

Eventually, integration started to take place in schools all over the country. Here, an African American student arrives at the University of Alabama to register for class.

the *Brown v. Board of Education* case, and the ruling changed the history of education in the country. It meant that white and African American children could now attend the same schools and have the right to the same level of education. Eventually, schools all over the United States began to integrate successfully.

Changes On Buses

Rosa Parks lived in Montgomery, Alabama. As an African American, she was used to taking a seat at the back of the bus, behind the seats on which white passengers sat. One day, in 1955, Rosa refused to give up her seat for a white passenger when there were no "white" seats left. She was promptly arrested, and thrown in jail. Civil rights organizations used her arrest to spur African Americans in Montgomery to boycott the city's buses. For more than a year, African Americans found other ways to get to work and to school. On November 15, 1956, the Supreme Court ruled that segregation on public transport was illegal, and the city desegregated the buses. This was another victory for civil rights.

Rosa Parks defended her civil rights when she refused to give up her seat on a Montgomery city bus. This statue of her was unveiled in the US Capitol's Statuary Hall, Washington, D.C., in 2013.

Asa Philip Randolph

Asa Philip Randolph was an important activist who worked to ban discrimination in the workplace. He was born in Florida in 1889, and moved to Harlem, New York City, to study economics and philosophy at City College. During World War I, he founded *The Messenger*, a magazine that campaigned for civil rights in the military and wartime industries.

Protecting Workers

After World War I, Randolph began to organize African American workers in laundromats, clothing factories, and movie theaters. In 1925, he became president of the Brotherhood of

Asa Philip Randolph helped bring about desegregation in the military, and was the director of the March on Washington for Jobs and Freedom.

Sleeping Car Porters (BSCP), and turned it into the first successful African American trade union. Randolph argued for employment opportunities for African Americans in the government and its industries.

Desegregating the Military

Randolph then organized the League for Nonviolent Civil Disobedience Against Military Segregation, and led protests calling for the complete desegregation of the military. In 1948, his work again achieved success when President Truman agreed to desegregate the United States' military forces.

Leading the March

In 1963, Randolph became involved in a protest march to Washington, called the March on Washington for Jobs and Freedom. He was director of the march, alongside Bayard Rustin. The march became one of the most momentous events in the American Civil Rights Movement.

The Brotherhood of Sleeping Car Porters was a trade union that protected the rights of porters on railways.

"It is hereby declared to be the policy of the president that there shall be equality of treatment and opportunity for all persons in the armed services without regard to race, color, religion, or national origin."
President Harry Truman, 1948.

Birmingham, Alabama

In the early 1960s, Birmingham, Alabama, was one of the most segregated of US cities. It had strong KKK influences and the chief police commissioner, Eugene Connor, was known for his racist views. Despite this, the American Civil Rights Movement was taking hold.

Racism had a strong hold in southern states such as Georgia and Alabama.

Washington, D.C.

ALABAMA
Birmingham
Montgomery
Atlanta
GEORGIA

Gathering Support

Aiming to end segregation, civil rights organizations rallied supporters and held protest marches and sit-ins across the city. Many African Americans were beaten and thrown in jail. One of those arrested on April 12, 1963, was Martin Luther King Jr., who took part as president of the SCLC.

The Children's March

In 1963, the SCLC decided to organize a march with hundreds of schoolchildren. The children marched in place of their parents, so they would not be arrested and lose their jobs. What happened next was shown on television and in newspapers around the world.

Attacking Children

The police arrested hundreds of children each day and used school buses to transport them to jail. Soon, the jails were full. Commissioner Connor then decided to use police dogs and water cannons against the peaceful protesters. It was an extreme show of violence, and the world was watching.

Young children were sprayed with water cannons during the protest. Some were even attacked and bitten by dogs.

The President Intervenes

President Kennedy was horrified by the events in Birmingham, and believed they had damaged the reputation of the United States. He put pressure on the white-owned businesses in the city to reach an agreement and, on May 10, businesses finally agreed to desegregate public facilities.

"The purpose of our direct-action program is to create a situation so crisis-packed that it will inevitably open the door to negotiation."
Martin Luther King Jr., in his Letter From a Birmingham Jail.

Randolph's dream of holding a mass protest in the capital was soon to become a reality. He started exchanging letters to organize a march. At the time, twice as many African Americans as white Americans were out of work, and those that were in work earned far less than their white colleagues.

Groups Come Together

After the events in Birmingham, the most important civil rights groups became more open to the idea of holding a mass march in Washington, D.C. The Student Nonviolent Coordinating Committee (SNCC), the Congress of Racial Equality (CORE), and SCLC were the first to show their support for the planned march.

Bayard Rustin (left), James Farmer (center right), and John Lewis (far right) were the leaders of influential civil rights groups.

These organizations strongly believed in nonviolent protest. Through peaceful sit-ins in public places and freedom rides on buses, the organizations had succeeded in changing segregation in the South. However, what Randolph really needed was the support of the oldest of civil rights organizations, the NAACP. The group gave their support, provided no laws would be broken. They were followed by the National Urban League.

President Kennedy

While the five organizations and Randolph were planning the march, President Kennedy appeared on television to say that the events in Birmingham were unacceptable. He also promised African Americans a strong civil rights bill.

"One hundred years of delay have passed since President Lincoln freed the slaves, yet their grandsons… are not fully free. And this nation…will not be fully free until all its citizens are free."
President Kennedy.

Powerful Leaders

The leaders of each civil rights organization and Asa Randolph became known as the "Big Six." They were John Lewis of SNCC, James Farmer of CORE, Martin Luther King Jr. of SCLC, Roy Wilkins of the NAACP, and Whitney Young Jr. of the National Urban League.

Kennedy Takes Action

As promised in his television appearance, President Kennedy sent a civil rights bill to Congress on June 19, 1963. If passed, it would end segregation in some public places and guarantee the right to vote.

Moving Forward

Although the civil rights bill was a step in the right direction, civil rights leaders knew that some white southern politicians would still be against it. The leaders decided the march would not only be for equal jobs and pay, but would also act as a support for the president's bill.

The president's brother, Robert Kennedy, speaks at a CORE rally in June 1963.

President Kennedy negotiates with the Big Six at the White House.

To the White House

When President Kennedy heard of the plans for the march, he was concerned. If the march led to violence, it would give the politicians an excuse not to vote for his civil rights bill. The president invited the Big Six to the White House, where he asked them to call off the march.

Forging Ahead

The Big Six refused to back down, and left the White House without the president's support. However, this did not prevent them from moving forward with the plans for the march. It was soon announced that the march would take place on August 28, 1963, and that its aim was "to offer a great witness to the basic moral principles of human equality and brotherhood."

"We want success in Congress, not just a big show at the Capitol. Some of these people are looking for an excuse to be against us."
President Kennedy, speaking to the Big Six.

The Big Six had less than two months to prepare for the march. Money had to be raised to pay for portable toilets, drinking fountains, and other supplies, as well as to fund the leaflets and banners for the march. The organizations chose Bayard Rustin, along with Asa Philip Randolph, to organize the event.

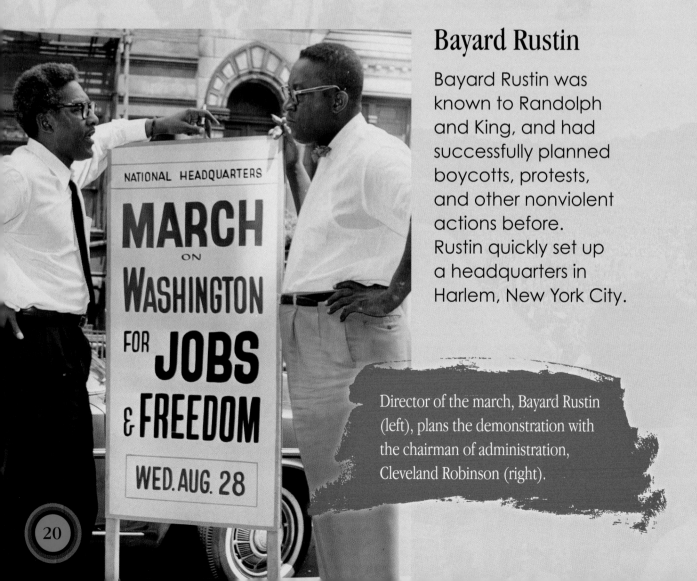

Bayard Rustin

Bayard Rustin was known to Randolph and King, and had successfully planned boycotts, protests, and other nonviolent actions before. Rustin quickly set up a headquarters in Harlem, New York City.

NATIONAL HEADQUARTERS

MARCH ON **WASHINGTON** FOR **JOBS** & **FREEDOM**

WED. AUG. 28

Director of the march, Bayard Rustin (left), plans the demonstration with the chairman of administration, Cleveland Robinson (right).

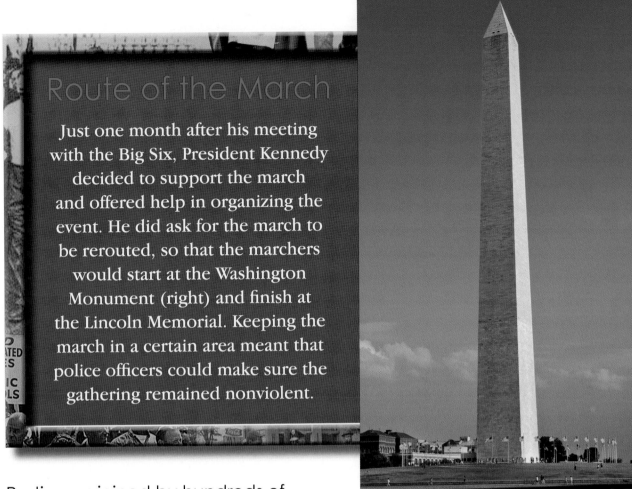

Route of the March

Just one month after his meeting with the Big Six, President Kennedy decided to support the march and offered help in organizing the event. He did ask for the march to be rerouted, so that the marchers would start at the Washington Monument (right) and finish at the Lincoln Memorial. Keeping the march in a certain area meant that police officers could make sure the gathering remained nonviolent.

Rustin was joined by hundreds of volunteers. The group designed, printed, and distributed flyers and leaflets. Rustin talked to newspapers, television and radio presenters, gave speeches, and even asked some celebrities to speak out and raise money for the march.

Raising Money

Each of the civil rights organizations helped with donations toward the costs, but more money was needed. The group decided to sell buttons promoting the march. The buttons showed a black and white hand clasped together. They were a huge success. More than 40,000 buttons were sold in just one month and helped to raise $15,000.

The March Begins

On August 28, buses, trains, planes, and cars from across the country started to arrive in Washington, D.C. Crowds of people, both white and African Americans, made their way on shuttle buses or walked to the Washington Monument.

Both white and African Americans took part in the March on Washington for Jobs and Freedom.

Music and Singing

By 9:30 a.m., more than 40,000 people had gathered at the Washington Monument. More than 200,000 had assembled by 11 a.m.! The crowds were entertained with songs by Joan Baez and Bob Dylan. A few hours later, and armed with signs that read "We Demand Equal Rights Now" and "We March for Jobs for All Now," the marchers made their way peacefully to the Lincoln Memorial.

Singers Joan Baez and Bob Dylan were among those that entertained the hundreds of thousands of marchers.

Some people sang freedom songs and some chanted "Freedom Now." Others simply remained silent.

"We will kneel-in, we will sit-in, until we can eat at any counter in the United States. We will walk until we are free." **Daisy Bates**.

Speeches to Inspire

By midday, more than 250,000 people had gathered at the mall between the monuments, waiting to hear the speeches. The event was broadcast all over the world. Randolph was one of the first to take the podium. Daisy Bates, the only woman speaker on the day, was next. She spoke of Rosa Parks and other women who had helped in the fight for civil rights. The speeches continued with John Lewis from the SNCC, a message from James Farmer of CORE, who was in jail at the time, Whitney Young Jr. of the National Urban League, and Roy Wilkins of the NAACP.

"I Have a Dream"

After many speeches, gospel singer Mahalia Jackson's powerful rendition of "How I Got Over" revived the marchers. Then, Randolph invited Martin Luther King Jr. to speak.

More than 250,000 Americans marched on Washington, D.C., on August 28, 1963.

"I have a dream that my four little children will one day live in a nation where they will not be judged by the color of their skin but by the content of their character. I have a dream today…."
Martin Luther King Jr.

Martin Luther King Jr.

King was probably the most famous of all the civil rights leaders because of his involvement in the Montgomery Bus Boycott and the protests in Birmingham. The marchers, and the world, listened as King spoke of his hopes and dreams for the future. King's "I Have a Dream" speech is one of the most important speeches in American history.

"... when all of God's children... will be able to join hands and sing... 'Free at last, free at last. Thank God Almighty, we are free at last.'"
Martin Luther King Jr.

The crowd cheered and cried as Martin Luther King Jr. delivered his famous speech to the marchers.

The Greatest Demonstration for Freedom

King started his speech saying that the March on Washington for Jobs and Freedom would go down in history as the greatest demonstration for freedom in the history of the nation. The march was exactly that, a defining moment in American history. After King's speech, Bayard Rustin read out a list of demands. They included an end to housing discrimination, programs to help unemployment, immediate desegregation, and the passing of Kennedy's civil rights bill.

The march was the largest single protest for civil rights that the United States had ever seen. It was an overwhelming success, with more than one-quarter of a million people gathering peacefully to protest for jobs and freedom for all. Nevertheless, it took time for people to notice any change in their daily lives.

Birmingham Bombing

Despite the march's huge success, most white southerners were still against Kennedy's civil rights bill, and violence continued in some areas. Just two weeks after the astounding march, KKK members planted a bomb at the 16th Street Baptist Church in Birmingham. The explosion injured many children, and killed four young girls. The nation was outraged, and many African Americans wondered if things would ever really change.

President Kennedy in Dallas, Texas, minutes before his assassination.

Death of the President

The civil rights bill was still being processed when President Kennedy was assassinated in November 1963. Some thought this might stop the civil rights bill from being signed, but Kennedy's successor, Lyndon B. Johnson, pushed the bill through. On July 2, 1964, the Civil Rights Act became law. Among those attending the signing were Martin Luther King Jr. and other civil rights leaders. It was a momentous occasion, and one that many African Americans thought might never happen.

Voting Rights Act

One year after the Civil Rights Act, the Voting Rights Act was also signed, which meant that all American citizens could vote without taking literacy tests. Life was still a battle for most African Americans, however. Many faced anger and abuse in the streets, and struggled to find work that was well paid. The civil rights organizations continued to fight for African Americans throughout the 1960s and onward, until, slowly, the lives of most African Americans started to improve.

Martin Luther King Jr. was present when President Lyndon B. Johnson signed the Civil Rights Act in 1964.

A Lasting Legacy

Bayard Rustin said the March on Washington for Jobs and Freedom was a march "to embody in one gesture civil rights as well as national economic demands." However, the march had a far greater impact than that.

A United Country

The march united people from all parts of the United States, both African Americans and white Americans. More than 250,000 people gathered together in one place to listen to some of the most significant leaders of the American Civil Rights Movement. These leaders inspired their followers, and the whole world was watching.

Martin Luther King Jr. was assassinated on April 4, 1968. Here, his widow, Coretta King, attends the burying of a time capsule in his honor in Washington, D.C.

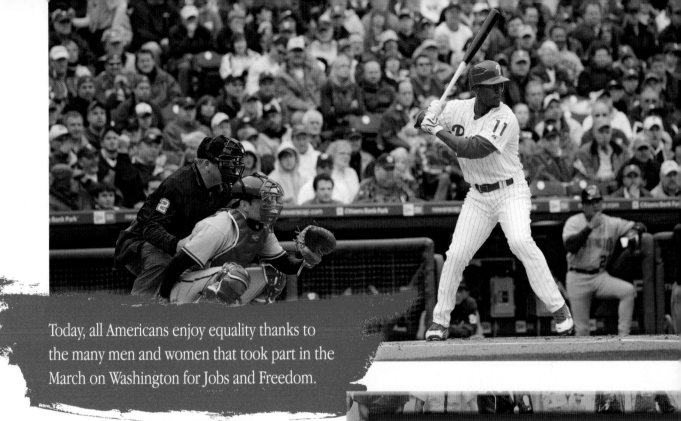

Today, all Americans enjoy equality thanks to the many men and women that took part in the March on Washington for Jobs and Freedom.

Freedom for All

The Big Six continued their work long after the march was over. Asa Philip Randolph formed the A. Philip Randolph Institute to fight poverty, with Bayard Rustin as the head of the organization. King, Wilkins, Young Jr., and James Farmer continued to fight for the civil rights cause.

Today, life for African Americans would be very different were it not for the March on Washington for Jobs and Freedom and the Big Six. These exceptional leaders inspired hundreds of thousands of Americans to come together and unite for one cause. Equality for all Americans is their legacy.

A Fitting Prize

In 1964, Martin Luther King Jr. received the Nobel Peace Prize for his work in the American Civil Rights Movement. At the age of 35, he was the youngest man to win the award. When King heard about the $54,123 prize, he said he would donate the money to the furtherance of the Civil Rights Movement.

Glossary

abolished (uh-BAH-lisht) Outlawed, made illegal.

boycott (BOY-kot) To refuse to use.

campaigned (kam-PAYN-d) Planned a series of actions to reach a particular goal.

cause (CAWZ) An idea or goal that many people are interested in.

challenge (CHA-lenj) To question the rightness of something.

civil rights (SIH-vul RYTS) The rights given by a government to all its citizens.

colleagues (KAH-leegz) People who have the same job or employer as others.

community (kuh-MYOO-nih-tee) A group of people who live close together or have shared interests.

desegregated (dee-SEH-gruh-gayt-ed) Stopped the use of separate schools and facilities for people of different races.

discrimination (dis-krih-muh-NAY-shun) Treating some people differently from others.

donations (doh-NAY-shunz) Money given toward something, such as a charity or a cause.

equal rights (ee-KWUL RYTS) The same rights for all people.

equality (ih-KWAH-luh-tee) Being equal.

exceptional (ek-SEP-shuh-nul) Outstanding, particularly good.

integrate (IN-tuh-grayt) To bring together, to mix.

military (MIH-luh-ter-ee) To do with the armed forces.

minister (MIH-nuh-stur) Someone who can perform or help at religious services.

pastor (PAS-tur) A minister or priest in charge of a church.

politicians (pah-lih-TIH-shunz) People who hold a political position in government.

racist (RAY-sist) The belief that a particular race of people are superior to another.

reputation (reh-pyoo-TAY-shun) How someone or something is viewed by people.

segregation (seh-gruh-GAY-shun) A system to keep white Americans and African Americans apart.

Supreme Court (suh-PREEM KORT) The highest court in the United States.

trade union (TRAYD YOON-yun) A union of workers who are skilled in a particular craft or trade.

unjustly (un-JUST-lee) Unfairly.

witness (WIT-nes) To watch or be present at.

Further Reading

Burgan, Michael. *John F. Kennedy*. Mankato, MN: Capstone Press, 2014.

Jeffrey, Gary. *Martin Luther King Jr. and the March on Washington*. A Graphic History of the Civil Rights Movement. New York: Gareth Stevens Learning Library, 2012.

Mis, Melody S. *Meet Martin Luther King Jr*. Civil Rights Leaders. New York: PowerKids Press, 2008.

Websites

Due to the changing nature of Internet links, PowerKids Press has developed an online list of websites related to the subject of this book. This site is updated regularly. Please use this link to access the list:
www.powerkidslinks.com/wso/march/

Index